CW01249895

The Whitby Rhymes

Alex Anderson ©copyright 2016 All Rights Reserved

The rights of Alex Anderson to be identified as the author of this work have been asserted in accordance with the Copyright, Designs and Patents Act 1988

All rights reserved. No part may be reproduced, adapted, stored in a retrieval system or transmitted by any means, electronic, mechanical, photocopying, or otherwise without the prior written permission of the author or publisher.

Spiderwize
Remus House
Coltsfoot Drive
Woodston
Peterborough
PE2 9BF

www.spiderwize.com

The views expressed in this work are solely those of the author and do not necessarily reflect the views of the publisher, and the publisher hereby disclaims any responsibility for them.

The Whitby Rhymes

By

Alex Anderson

Dedicated to the loving Memory of

ANTHONY & RITA COONEY

.

"There is no shame in sorrow."

CONTENTS.

African Sequence – 9

The Land & The Sea – 18

Nomad – 19

Jericho – 20

Scenes from the Via Lucis – 21

Give us This Night – 31

The Tree – 32

The Ferryman – 33

The Whitby Rhymes. I – XX – 34

Pilgrimage – 50

The Wood Carver (of Bethlehem) – 52

Cathedral – 52

God's Raiment – 54

Parable – 55

Credo – 57

Offertory – 60

To End a Nightmare – 61

This is the Stone – 62

And Silence Spoke That Name – 64

And Desert was Begat – 67

Disquiet – 68

The Oracle – 69

Holy Rock – 71

Melchizedek – 72

A Celtic Christmas – 74

Child of My Joy – 75

The Christening Party – 76

One Hundred Names – 77

Guilty – 78

The Vase – 80

This Wind – 81

The Magus – 82

Omega – 83

The War Room – 85

The Prophet – 94

The Shaman – 95

Xerophilus – 96

African Harvest – 97

Ashes – 107

Denial – 108

The Garment – 109

The Nine Days of St. Anthony – 112

The Birth Stone – 117

AFRICAN SEQUENCE.

What do you see?

I see a woman sitting in the shade.

What do you see?

I see a woman sitting in the shade

of trees that stand together in white sand.

What do you see?

I see a woman sitting in the shade

of trees that stand together in white sand,

whose skin is black

whose robes are bright with all the colours

of the earth, and about whose neck

are beads of purple, red and green.

...

What do you see?

I see a woman sitting in the shade

of trees that stand together in white sand,

whose skin is black

whose robes are bright with all the colours

of the earth, and about whose neck

are beads of purple, green and red.

I see her sit with brightly coloured

straws that flow like rivulets

between her nimble hands

to join the flood and river

of the mat she weaves.

I see a pattern form among the weave:

of one hand pointing to the sand

of one hand pointing to the lips

of one hand pointing to the sky

from whence comes all the cattle of the earth.

What do you see?

I see a pattern form among the weave:

of one hand pointing to the sand

of one hand pointing to the lips

of one hand pointing to the sky,

from whence comes all the cattle of the earth.

...

I see among the weave

a pattern of the cattle of the earth

gathered at a single water hole,

a single herdsman watches over them

and all belong together

at the pool

Look again. What do you see?

I see at last the straws are running out,

the flood and flow of mats grows less

and gaps have spoilt the pattern and the weave.

Soon there will be no more,

a woman sitting in the shade of trees

that stand together in white sand,

whose skin is black,

and from whose nimble hands

the weave once rose and fell

as rivers flowing onward to the sea.

Today, my captive brother,

it is I

-who sits beside you weeping

in the dust

-who sits in fear beneath

the Ngap tree

-who leans against its twisted bole

-who speaks not out

for fear that tongue

betray the rebel

in this cheap commodity

here marketed and labelled

with a price amid the spices

and the unwashed dates.

The frightened merchandise

who waits to see

the unredeeming ransom changing hands,

and know the terror

of the bought and sold.

...

Today, my captive brother,

it is I, who sits beside you,

weeping in the dust.

Like you, my brother,

driven from the plains.

Like you, my own land calls me back

where none dare go.

Like you, I am the hunted

and the prey,

the fool who squandered

all his trust

upon the untrustworthy.

Like you, I keep the burden and the stain

of some forgotten sin

that somehow binds us all.

And it must be that Christ

has risen not,

that we still keep the

Stigma of the Fall.

What do you see?

Are your eyes awake?

I see a tree. The tree is Africa.

Her roots run deep and bind

one generation to the next;

beneath its leaves we shelter

from the fierce heat of the day.

Africa is not for you to study.

We gather not as slaves

nor heirs of slaves, but free;

as men of Africa come freely

from the turmoil of the past.

Africa is not for you to sell.

...

In our beloved and our ravaged land

we lift our heads, we taste the wind,

we judge if it be wind or rain

that drives away what you have ushered in.

Africa is not for you to pillage.

All the fears and perils of the bush,

the sad purveyors of adversity,

the futile remedies of those who

seek not Africa to know her ways,

are all but now a language of dissenting wrath

made still – an old skin sloughs away.

An African is not a man like you.

HE IS A MAN LIKE ME !

I look down deep into the pool of Africa

-the mirror of the world -

and see the man who is myself

look back at me.

Rejoice with me ! Your eyes are open now !

The woman weaves the tribes together

in her hands, like many coloured straws

they flow into the pattern of a Land.

THE LAND IS AFRICA.

The Pattern is Restored.

THE LAND AND THE SEA.

I hear you, Sea.

Will you be calm and listen now to me?

The Sea replies:

Why should I, feeble Man?

I am Who Am,

but you will scarcely be.

———

Grain has risen from the ground

as legends rise, and liturgies.

But at the outset of the world

it was not so,

the start of sacredness predates all men,

the land alone is holy.

NOMAD.

Yobel says that we have stayed too long:

the goats are thin,

the wells have failed,

the tents have settled in the sand.

Bless us, Lord, and do not let

your nomad roam forever,

but fasten us

with – chain to bind us

with – rope to tether us

with – cord to draw us in

with your strong hand

to hold us fast,

from all our wanderings.

JERICHO

Pilgrims laid their namelessness

before him

and he cured them.

One by one, he named them

to themselves,

he named them to their presence,

and they cowered in the world no more;

yet they envied him

and schemed against him.

Their child-like hearts went out of them,

and he, not wishing to deny them

pilgrimage, sent them forth again,

and gave them back

their nameless insignificance.

SCENES FROM THE VIA LUCIS.

Light from Light – from Tomb –

From *lux aeterna* shining out

of Darkness come as hoped for

promise rolling back from ground

to seed – to stem – to bloom –

to unapproachable - to brilliance

    to Christ restored

    - LUX MUNDI –

    Light of all the World.

II.

A rolled up piece of cloth emits

a mirror image of the nails,

the flails, the seeping blood,

the sweat of suffering, the open

side, a death endured unto

the triumph of the cross.

Do not look for him among

the dead, he is not here,

He goes before you into Galilee.

III.

Tell me, Sir, are you the gardener?

On this dry piece of ground,

beside the empty sepulchre,

the healing herb, wild *Clear Eye,*

grows the best, though some

have called it *Eye of Christ,*

because it purifies the sight

of all who seek the Remedy.

IV.

Beloved Stranger, bless to us

the desert road, the day long spent.

In breaking bread, lift over us

your wounded hands and bless

to us those patriarchs who walked

in hope of you, who stood with

you upon your holy mountain,

    bathed in light.

Stiffen our resolve, sanctify and

bless to us The Risen Man.

V.

Was that the Ghost of Galilee,

who sat beside an inland sea,

and from the shore called out to me?

Who baked a fish upon a fire?

A Ghost who breathed a small suspire;

broke the fish, to my surprise,

and ate it there, before my eyes?

VI.

Pay to me one peppercorn of praise,

so small a price for all you have

received: the power to forgive the

jollity of sin, the merriment of flawed

companionship, the seven spears

thrust daily in my side, the power

to restore the upturned chalice

and the scattered loaves.

The one prince of this world,

who knows defeat, will not

surrender, but to the seven

salves I leave to you.

VII.

If some should say to you:

Come seek the Lord,

do not look for him in secret

places out of sight and hidden,

to await a day when some shall

flock to him to hear great

bursts of oratory, and calls

to rise up as the army of a king.

.

It is not so. He walks at peace

among us. I saw him in plain sight,

and I give testimony

HE ALONE IS THIS - THE SON OF GOD.

VIII.

The voice of Babel calls from many towers:

- it cannot mean the same because –

- language has evolved – original Hebrew –

- original Greek – original Aramaic –

-Semitic verb – Canaan dialect –

- mistranslation – semantics –

Thomas, doubt no more. Follow the men

who follow the Christ,

His Saints and Martyrs.

IX.

Up from the portico of Earth,

Triumphant Christ has risen to the Father.

He has not left to us a festival

of last farewells, an emptiness of orphans,

   abandoned and bereft of Hope.

    He is the Risen One

   we know him by his wounds.

X.

Going, therefore, teach all clowns

and mountebanks – acrobat and idler-

charlatan – prelate - cut purse and deceiver

of the poor – honest and dishonest men alike,

and all who say they do not know the Lord .

From high and low, go seek them out

and teach them of the feast I have

prepared for them. Compel them in,

this stubborn race of men who will

not dance as David did, before the

    Altar of the Lord.

GIVE US THIS NIGHT...

conformity with water

except where a flower closes

in a subtle shift of light

conformity with air

except in that fearful cloudburst

of again migrating wings

conformity with fire

except where the entrails of the earth

condemn our tactless consanguinity

conformity with dreams

except where the pagan faltered

and lacking vision

ate his fill.

THE TREE.

At that same hour, going out,

again she found the tree.

The burning faggot breaks its bonds,

and out of earth`s dark core

a black blood courses upwards

with such grief, where hangs a man

upon a witches` tree.

Then placing to her lips

the ripened fruit, she cried aloud:

I know you, Tree.

And still rejoicing thus,

did call upon the hanging man

to share her great discovery.

THE FERRYMAN.

Because, I could not pay the ferryman,

he would not carry me, and poured

contempt on this small purse of prayer

and penances I offered as a ransom,

had hoped to bargain with among

the other shades, not knowing until

then, how worthless was my specie.

Wiser now, I stand with

outstretched hand

beneath the Cross,

a mendicant,

a beggar for His mercy.

The Whitby Rhymes. I – XX.

(Broadly based on a notion of some Saxon originals).

High in the mountains of the Lord,

a stream begins, a spring of cleansing

water trickles down the rock that is our faith.

We, who are begotten of the torrent

and redeemed in Christ, are called

to walk upon a turbulence of tides,

into the outstretched arms of God.

II.

God mourns with his people;

tears of men and angels flow

down all the cracks and crevices

of unforgiving lands, where now

the one prince of this world

has led a faithless nation.

III.

I ask it Lord, I do not sin today.

I call upon two trees to witness me.

I call upon two lamps to light my way.

I call upon the naked pebble stone:

Cast not thyself at me for sinfulness.

IV.

I take upon my back:

the Flails of Christ –

the Nails of Christ –

the Wood of Christ –

the Blood of Christ –

I take upon my back today,

the Cross of Christ,

that He may not so fall

beneath the weight of it.

V.

It walks about in darkness,

the business of the night.

In fear I lie awake, alert,

and draw about myself

the amulets of Christ:

> a ring of light
>
> a ring of beads
>
> a ring of tears
>
> a ring of prayer

arranged around me

arranged around me.

VI.

Send me too, O Lord

into your vineyard,

at harvest time

at planting time

    on quiet days

    on unquiet days

and set me to your work.

VII.

Bride of the seven sorrows,

Bride of the seven straws,

walk with me a while – a while

    upon bare feet

    upon hard grass

    among the stones

    among the flints

with those who follow Him

with those who follow Him.

VIII.

I pray aloud the God

of earth and water.

I pray aloud the God

of wind and sea.

I pray aloud the God

of woods and hollows.

Why does He

not hear, nor answer me?

IX.

Brother Sun, do not betray me,

   give me but your warmth.

Sister Moon, do not deceive me,

   give me but your light.

Brother Fish, among the shallows,

   give me but your word.

Brother Goat, I send into the desert,

   carry not my sins away,

   for they alone are mine.

X.

If, in spring, the light of Christ

should lengthen with the days,

to warm my soul anew and loosen

all the bounden strings that keep

me back from pilgrimage,

then will I walk the three times

round my house and back again,

to thank the Lord of Days who

keeps me in this place

  that I may serve him

  that I may serve him.

XI.

O, tiny rose so red, where late He bled,

take not upon thyself His blood

but let it at the flood flow over us.

Cloud burst break upon the light

of He who is my soul's delight,

and all that falls as crimson rain

mark ever with a crimson stain

we sheaves of all the dead.

XII.

See how I wander in the wilderness,

and yet I am not orphaned in your sight.

In faith and in the midst of all my wanderings

I travel still to that last place

where you have summoned me.

Or, is it just a tale told by the wind,

a song made up of dried out leaves,

a gentle soughing of disturbed sand;

no more than move towards my final end,

    my last annihilation?

XIII.

You, the Potter, Lord, I but the clay.

From the earth you take me.

From the earth you break me.

Over and over you take me.

Over and over you break me,

shatter and remake me, until

the nothing left of me held

in your hand becomes the all

your purpose and your will of me.

XIV.

The breath of God, unborn,

moved on the waters,

the torrent stream began.

Not as Vltava or Thames,

an unsure trickle rising in

the hills, but at the full,

in spate, in steady flow

there came the long eternal

prayer of God, made man.

XV.

Each breath I take and

each beat of my heart

    belongs to God,

for I am His possession.

And of His other gifts to me,

what have I done with them

but hidden them in hollows,

in the depths of woods,

deep buried them in sand,

for I have in His sight

flawed each of them.

XVI.

Here shall I sit and sing;

turning back the surge

of tides that break upon

the shore of wilderness, echoes

of eternity bereft of sound.

Sweet silence, it is not you I dread,

but He whose voice may call me

out to tread the same path He

processed along to Calvary.

XVII.

How deep, the mysteries of God,

and how profound His ways.

Who is there among the sons

of men can know them all?

From our first gasp of life, until

the last, we are ensnared in God,

in trap, in gin sprung shut,

in days we cast about with no

hope of release from that dread hand;

the hunter's purpose closed to us.

XVIII.

I make my prayer to the Godhead Three

    God of God who made me

    Son of God who saved me

Ghost of God who said: *COME FOLLOW ME.*

XIX.

Your servant, Lord, am I. At this

first hour of the day I come to hear your word.

Perhaps you could speak up a bit,

or wave a hand, or even

still the voice of this loud foghorn priest

whose holy yells disturb the

alcoves of the church,

and deafen me

to what you ask of me?

XX.

Three things are these

that be not ever ending:

the Peace of God

the Love of God

the Everlasting Mercy.

PILGRIMAGE

The Love of God

is song to me

and leads me ever on -

is sun to me

and shade to cover me

is bread to me

and water to my thirst

is cloak to me

and strong shoes to my feet

is staff to me

that I may lean upon.

The Love of God

Is road to me

and goes before me

into Paradise.

THE WOOD CARVER.

(of Bethlehem).

Carved from the wood of the olive tree,

    the persecuted Christ.

Carved is the land where Christ has walked.

Carved is the shade where Christ has talked.

    carved – is the stable of his birth

    carved – is the cradle of the earth

    carved – are the beads of Mary`s fears

    carved – that we may count her tears

    carved – is the image of the Cross

    carved – is the gain that came from loss

    Carved is the world of God`s reflection,

    Carved is the hope of Resurrection.

CATHEDRAL.

What say we to each? What proclamation

make? What visitation do we blunder in upon

that has the auger of unlikely Birth?

What promise is fulfilled and present come

to pose more questions than we care to heed?

A dove set down and gave the answer thus:

New wine flows best around a wedding feast,

    accept – the banquet is for you –

Transfigured light has fallen on the meal,

break your bread and share it openly.

Anticipate the worse, and it will come:

    a flail has brought us low,

a crown has pierced us with its mockery,

    beneath a weight of wood

we stumble on towards no final end.

On this fair morning, rise we up anew

and turn our gaze towards the parting

clouds – we feel a breath of wind –

the Pilot of our Faith has gone aboard,

that we may sail the barque of Christ

    towards eternity.

The Stone rejected has become the Cornerstone.

GOD`S RAIMENT.

the Sun

who in his heart has said

-*I AM NOT GOD*-

still gives his light in all the darkened places;

the Rain

who in her heart has said

-*I AM NOT GOD*-

still raises up the harvest of our lives;

the Wind

who in his heart has said

-*I AM NOT GOD*-

still drives for us the great sails of the nations;

the Earth

who in her heart has said

-*I AM NOT GOD*-

still bears upon her back

the sorrows of the land.

Praise – All Praise

The Beauty of the Lord, who makes of them

a raiment for Creation, and robes in splendour

this infected isle.

PARABLE.

The first, I buried in the ground, for this is memory,

all metal bright,

though ended are the dynasties.

Hard struck, the edges of my sun drenched days

come down with tapping sounds to these abodes,

like blind men seeking with their canes

the place where Ra sleeps fitfully,

his head laid on his oars.

The second, I have always carried with me,

for this is guilt,

accrued with interest, where pagans opened

all their gates to me and I, a pilgrim,

feasted in their land.

Where she gave unto me and I did eat

as from a long estrangement, called to prayer,

except there is no hope of journey ended,

and her breasts are gall.

...

The third, I traded at a loss, for this is peace,

my white plumed bird

who once sat candle still beside my head.

Her songs, like darts of light

about the corners of my room,

have seeped through cracks and doors

to unknown tribes, who now placate false gods

upon strange altar stones.

CREDO.

I believe in Poetry:

the first created Oneness of the Word,

arising from the darks and deeps

of God`s eternal energies.

Let me go down into the entrails of the earth,

renew me there and let me live again

that moment when his nostrils brought to life

the first pulsations of that holy fire,

now poets in their generations nurture

all too briefly

in the intervals of passing hand to hand.

...

I believe in Poetry:

the great vibrating soul possessing me

and filling me with wonders.

For he has loosed the bound strings

of my tongue, that I may speak.

Yet covers me with suppurating sores

and leprosy, so men avoid my gaze and cast me out,

and though I shout aloud my singing words,

they turn from me and stopping up their ears

they hear me not, nor answer me.

I believe in Poetry: The fearful Being

God sends forth

to stalk his open spaces.

He makes of me a bond slave

to his Stillness,

the great weight of his hand restrains me there.

He takes my futile strength into his Vastness,

and sends to me

the Terror of his Word.

OFFERTORY.

This is my body:

beneath his loving hand

my bone and sinew now

are scattered carrion.

This is my blood:

the wounding stream not stilled

but evermore made one with sand,

where dogs have sought to feed upon my soul

yet failed in their malevolence.

Who now can keep his tears to himself

when crows are nesting

in the olive trees?

TO END A NIGHTMARE.

He

who seeks release from evil dreams,

throwing off the burden of his fear

among a sanctuary of leaves,

let him hold aloft his hands

and spread his fingers as it were a vine.

Soon

will he find the odours of his dread

grow sweetly scented in the branches there,

and if, for incantation, he intones

the fullness of the undivided self in whispers,

this too will save him.

THIS IS THE STONE.

This is the stone we seek to understand,

to know where all things have their place,

appointed place;

for stones must not be moved, mislaid, lifted,

set aside, nor smuggled from the beach

to cause division and disorder.

What seems a pebble from the beach, a stone

a long way from the shore, must still be proved

so that the pebble be restored, returned,

replaced where order has decreed it best belongs.

This is the stone we carry to the water's edge,

to prove the origin of pebbles is the sea,

the origin of pebbles is the sea,

to hold it carefully where sea-wet sand will test

the workmanship to prove the origin of pebbles

is the sea.

If this should fail and still the pebble is not altered,

worn down, changed, corrupted or decayed,

or simply rendered different from what

it has become, then we have still

to learn the place where sand begat the stone

we now must ponder with our failed philosophies.

AND SILENCE SPOKE THAT NAME.

Nothing came first:

Nothing was aware of Nothing and spoke its name,

it spoke the name of Nothing

and Nothing was.

Stillness came next:

Nothing was aware of Stillness and spoke its name,

it spoke the name of Stillness

and Stillness was.

Night came next:

Stillness was aware of Night and spoke its name,

it spoke the name of Night

and so Night was.

Day came next:

Night was aware of Day and spoke its name,

it spoke the name of Day

and so Day was.

And the Day spoke:

it asked the Name of He who names all things,

and Chaos answered Chaos in reply

and Chaos was.

And Chaos was:

Chaos spoke the name of Night and Darkness was.

Chaos spoke the name of Stillness and Clamour was;

and out of clamour came forth voices

and out of voices came forth anger

and out of anger came forth deafness

and out of deafness came forth Silence

and Silence was.

...

And Silence was:

and out of Silence came

the Name of He

who names all things

And Silence spoke that Name.

And Silence spoke that Name.

Then He who names all things, named Chaos

The Accursed.

And Stillness was restored

and Night was

and the Day.

And Silence was.

And Silence was the Avatar of God.

AND DESERT WAS BEGAT.

The fig tree was not yet, nor was the vine.

Of sand, was still the darkness on the deep.

Of sand the rivers ran, of sand the sea,

And sand it was that battered at the rock

To call forth sand on sand abundantly.

In syllables of sand the Earth lay still

An inarticulate and ancient dust, until

The feet of Rham caused words to rise

In life-clouds bearing all the names

That sand at last would utter to the ground.

Then sand knew sand, and desert was begat.

The One in whom alone there is no lie.

Who holds the cup and scourges the unwary.

The One named, Purity of Place, the Foundling Self,

The Silence Quickens,

And Death Sings Quietly.

DISQUIET.

We are a desperate and a shabby people;

we measure out our hasty angers,

our petty imbecilities.

We search about us for some new Pretender,

whose specious alchemy of claims

can set aside this senile earth, or this,

the last of our most empty hopes,

allay the threats of Heaven and Hell

and unimaginative Limbo.

We are a pagan and unhappy people.

Where is the comfort

we can bring each other,

whilst the fabric of our trivial assent

has settled on the upturned face of Arles?

THE ORACLE.

The Oracle, especially in Spring,

is programmed to respond, so that

to eat

to drink

to procreate

to get

to run from risk, are laws of times and seasons

fixed in the cycle of the spheres,

immutably.

The Pilgrim too has energies;

a mess of grey stuff mixed with blood,

so contradictory

so uncontrolled

he falters in his search to know

the music of the spheres,

to hear it chime with such profundity

he will not wish to speak of it.

...

Pilgrim, you have travelled

far enough to have your prejudice confirmed

(it is the Oracle who speaks)

know this instead, that men have preached

to fishes long enough,

now perhaps should fishes preach to men.

HOLY ROCK.

It is as though the land, through centuries,

brought forth a worthless shrine;

a needlessly assembled shape of stones

erected into cairns and dominations,

a place to venerate the remade gods.

It is as though a faith were scribbled onto leaves,

with rites, processions, hardships for a journey into grace;

not left to lie wind drifted, pressed

and gathered up, these sacramentals hidden

from the eyes of simple piety, ignored and chained

with superstition and the holy rule.

It is as though the wind, clear northerly,

cold seeped into the mortar of the walls, prayer laden.

Wind-drift stopping up the mouths of priests.

The last solemnity of candles flowing out

not sanctity but tallow, so ended there

such deeds as men once called religion.

MELCHIZEDEK.

Like Mechizedek of old;

except that he,

the song gone from his lips,

the bread and wine grown stale,

stands mute, uncertain where to turn,

and none to tell him where the dead have gone.

The dead

the innocents

the vanished ones

who now on this third day

descended into hell

for their beliefs and unbeliefs,

await compassion like a shaft of light

to fall in all the darkened places.

We fill twelve baskets

with the remnants of our prayers

and send them out again, except that they,

confronted by so many roads that end

in blank walls and despair,

bring back to us,

though crucified and dead,

the Ever-Living Names

of Freedom.

A CELTIC CHRISTMAS.

Bless to me, Sweet Bride,

Sweet ribbons from the loom

Sweet pebbles from the shore

Sweet shells alive with light,

My little bread and wine.

Bless to me, Sweet Bride,

My stable ted with straw

Where comes a tired man

Grown gaunt,

Who leads upon an ass

A tired woman, heavily with Child.

CHILD OF MY JOY.

Child of my joy, where do you hide from me?

Are you beneath the rubble of a counting house,

or in a drain among such rats

as fight with you for food?

Perhaps, imprisoned in a world of graceless men,

you weep alone?

Where are you now, who slept at peace

upon your mother`s arm,

when first I saw you there, in Bethlehem?

THE CHRISTENING PARTY.

Blessed be the Ark that paused for her.

Blessed be the loving hands that

lifted her aboard the Raft of God`s great mercy.

Blessed be the God

who walked among us, sat with us

and laughed all our jokes.

Blessed be the God of all Beatitudes.

Blessed too, the God of such good humour;

the Devil hath not merriment

the likes of this.

ONE HUNDRED NAMES.

The land has many names

for men to muse upon,

the Earth speaks only of

herself and of her wonders.

My little cat ignores me

when I call, though ponders

on the name she gave herself.

And, later on today when I go out,

the camels all will spit at me,

and joke among themselves

    I do not know

the Hundred Names of God.

GUILTY.

My sin goes round the world.

It flies up like a cheerful bird

on bright defiant wings. It flaps

and flutters in the face of God,

and taunts the Everlasting Mercy.

A soaring burst of song, it lifts

and lilts and flies where slave

ships ride at anchor, loading

cargo off the coast of Senegal.

Where gypsy fiddles play their

merry notes, it hovers in the blackened

air among tall chimneys belching

forth the stench of death.

My sin goes round the world.

The innocent, the unborn dead sing

not again, for they hang up their

harps in unkind lands.

THE VASE.

Abba, in the wilderness I have not found

the things you promised me, but only these:

a swirl of sand, a tree of leaves that

rattle in the breeze, a heated wind,

a place where water lies so deep, both

men and camels come upon their knees

to drink of it; and manna is not there.

Why have you offered me an empty jar?

If you would live at peace

among the sands, plunge your hands down

deep into the vase, the desert's vastness

and its emptiness, find there and lift from it

those things our God has stored for you.

THIS WIND ...

This wind, from whence does it

come to shake the olive trees?

Arising from these paving stones

perhaps, hard baked beneath

the feet of passing patriarchs?

Or, has the Spirit sent his breath

once more, to sanctify and cool

for us this midday air?

THE MAGUS.

Not in itself the journey, do I fear,

a pilgrim way through forests

filled with caution and unease;

not from itself the Sanctus,

    do I hide,

a tocsin chiming in a land

not sick of journeying.

Rather do I dread a sudden fall

among the burning curse of arid

places, the boundless desert

of a total faith; a fear that from the

tension of the flames, in reaching out,

I touch the banished Christ.

OMEGA.

The Stone Man stepped

out of the mountainside,

whole and entire.

And in the shattered

pieces of his afterbirth,

we honoured him among

ourselves for those few

things he granted us.

The Iron Man has promised

us, all wisdom will be ours,

all miracles made known, the

nature of all things laid plain

before us. With him we will

renew the face of all the Earth

and have no godly image

    but our own.

                  ...

The Green Man planted first

the tree, did worship it —

(Eternal — Summer — Come)

did make its leaves to clothe

the naked woman and the man,

did sprinkle it with wine, did

take its ripened fruit, did lie

awake beneath it in the shade.

The Man of Stone

Is weathered into sand.

The Iron Man

Is dust upon the land.

The Man of Green we

worshipped with the trees —

an end of these,

for nothing has sufficed where

now the last Man standing,

      is The Christ.

THE WAR ROOM.

He has furnished me with arrows

and bids me do his will, where now

great gates have grown up from

the ground, and all men have become

my enemy. So too, I dread the tiger

and the snake, all things that move

in water, inhabit land or fill the

screaming air; flowers of the field

are fear to me, the trees all stride

toward me, fitted out for war, aloud

with menacing. So many erstwhile

friends were these who now are all become

such enemies and seek my fall.

...

Paradise denied? A gate stands closed?

A cherub with a flaming sword? *Theatrical!*

What is all of this to me? I, who fully know

the measure of all things a jealous God

restrains in me. *What vanity! What pride!*

    The Serpent spoke the truth:

You are not dead, but live and draw

upon yourself the garment of divinity.

At last are free to know that rank

and pomp and praise and high esteem

can all be yours. Today you cast aside

the yoke of crass humility and are

become as those, who like myself,

are set apart – an aristocracy of all

    who disobey.

Count upon your beads the names

of anger: a dung heap smouldering,

an old man sat with venom in his nose,

spittle falling from the lips of discontented

wives, endless dripping from an unsound

roof, a leaking water jar, a winter fireside

bringing not its warmth, but immolation.

The edict of the Mameluke holds firm,

and he has cast me out with fearful rage.

...

He watched her walk a labyrinth

of eucalyptus trees; in and out

of shadow saw her move;

now seen – now gone again.

And he declaimed his poem

loudly to the trees. He said:

Do not hide her from my view,

nor from my vision shield her,

nor separate from me the sight

of she most dear, but let mine

eyes alight on one who does not

know me, or how my lust will rage

unto the grave.

Thou shalt not covet thy neighbour's wife,

nor ox, nor ass, nor field of olive trees.

Thou shalt not wish thyself to be the sand

about her feet, the breeze that teases her,

nor yet the stream wherein she stands to

bathe and there embrace her nakedness.

Thou shalt not place thy kiss on her soft

lips and there remain. Seek not thy redemption

in her arms, nor in the laying on of hands,

        thine absolution.

...

Barley yields are up, and so is oil,

the surplus wheat will have to go

in store, the price may rise. The steady

upward cost of wine denies it to the

lax impious poor. *Have they not water?*

New clothes are plentiful again, and

none go barefoot who can pay for shoes.

Who is there accuses me of greed?

My wealth and all I own belongs to God.

I pledged it all from birth. My barley,

wheat and oil I hold in store for Him.

My friend, I mourn with you, because

I cannot help you in your need.

Speak, Lord!

I hear your Holy Voice above the thunder.

But wait!

Was that a droplet on the window pane?

Are all the roads still wet? Will there be rain?

Is that a leaf I just saw moving in the breeze?

A great storm comes. I see it in the trees.

I am your wakeful watchman in the night.

But wait!

What of my new field? My oxen at the

plough? My orchard too, the olives ready now?

What of my wife, the she whom I must please?

You know how I must follow her decrees.

Am I not an old man, who may fall?

May even dash myself against a stone?

From your persistent call I haste away,

that I may heed your Voice some other day.

...

Do not call him back from rest,

but envy him with dirge and

muffled drum. Resent the votive

fire made of prayer; the king

of wood is dead, let him remain

and do not honour him.

Envy this libation of a life

now dribbled out to death,

to straw man sitting at a

window pane, to winding

cloth that moves upon the

breath of those who feign

to grieve and cast an unwet

eye upon a lost companion

welcomed home to joy.

Is this the wealth I have so sinned

to gain – this bitter fruit – these futile

darts – this fatal disobedience?

I stand upon a field of war where

still unburied lie the angry dead,

and here in sorrow plead for my release.

> *For my strong house of brick,*
>
> *On me, Sweet Lord, have mercy.*
>
> *For my full store of food,*
>
> *On me, Sweet Lord, have mercy.*
>
> *For water running cleanly, at my call,*
>
> *On me, Sweet Lord, have mercy.*
>
> *For Bread that is your Body.*
>
> *For Wine that is your Blood.*
>
>   *For all your Holy Word*
>
> *Come freely to my hearing,*
>
> *On me, Sweet Lord, have mercy.*

THE PROPHET.

Singer of psalms and carrier of fleas,

you spread your unmarked charts before us all;

you offer us new landfalls made of old desires.

The laurel has become a burning bush

of deep disturbing dreams,

or so you claim.

See you not, how caravans of pilgrims still arrive

from towns that did not heed your words,

what use had they for your crude patronage?

The lodestone does not swing nor point away

from what we surely know of boundaries,

why do you still offend us with wild cries?

THE SHAMAN.

Blue are the waters of the lough

and white, white the sail.

The sun shines fitfully,

the clouds have promised rain.

And what must I, the Shaman, make of this?

Read into it?

Towards what sacred rock, what grove of speaking

leaves must I, in failing faith, repair?

What spirit of the febrile earth inhabit me?

Today, I beg, ask not of me what all this

means for peace or war,

for coming desolation and despair.

Blue are the waters of the lough

and white, white the sail.

The sun shines fitfully,

the clouds have promised rain.

XEROPHILUS.

He is a lover of deserts,

and is despised for it.

His pride he throws behind him

in the sand, he who casts aside

his purse, no longer weeps

for lost necessities.

Where none but he may go,

he wanders undisturbed,

and feels the sun in benediction

fall upon the desert

of a boundless world.

AFRICAN H A R V E S T.

Be still, my thoughts, and listen to the Silence:

between one tolling bell stroke and the next

between the Accusation and the Judgement

between the Judgement and the Crucifixion

between the Sorrow and the Death of Hopefulness

there comes

The Silence and the Silence.

She carries water 7 miles a day. Her name

Sweet One becomes *The Water Bearer*

and she, the first time, falls beneath its weight

Little girl, I say to you – Arise !

Source of Joy, I say to you – Wake Up !

...

They carried her on planks of cedar wood,

not in the clean fresh linen of her tribe;

she was not mourned, nor did the village

women do their dance, or dress in robes.

They took her to the outside of the town

and left her in her unclean flesh to lie

until some passing stranger might take

pity on her nothingness, and fold her

in the sand for all eternity.

Elijah blessed the jar –

        and there was oil:

Elijah blessed the grain –

        and there was bread.

Child, forgive your Mother –

Mother, forgive your Son –

The jars are stolen, and the meal is gone.

TWO.

Voices carried on the wind, all say:

A great land dies when good men hide

    away in shelters made

of straw, soon blown about in squalls,

or drifted in the dunes` forgetfulness.

Leave them behind, these men

who fiddle with the entrails of the past;

below the wet sand and the dry, dig deep,

a Great Land sings her stubborn song anew.

...

I came upon a eucalyptus tree

and asked of her: Give me a way

of seeing that is new, let there be

a pattern in the leaves that I can

lay as template on such forms

as are familiar and old, to wrest

from them the shape of things

    that will be different.

And of the cypress tree, I asked:

Give me your smallest branch

that's filled with sap, that I may

write upon your leaves such words

the wind will gather up and send

among those men who hold all

    leaves as dear.

THREE.

His mother walks all day,

the dead weight of her child

upon her back, and she no

longer feels the gentle rise

and fall his breathing made.

The cloth she wrapped about

him days ago, lets through

the smell of his small death.

Perhaps they will not notice

at the feeding place, and give her

rations for the both of them.

...

Sir,

Give me shelter from the rain,

and do not take it back again.

Give me perhaps a fishing boat,

a fat hen or a nanny goat.

Bid the goat give milk and cheese,

perhaps a kid too, if you please.

A hive of bees, a comb of honey,

that I can trade for petty money.

If you should find my voice too shrill,

and none of this shall be your will,

then give me just a tiny fish

or butter in a wooden dish,

that I may go upon my way

and not beg in the streets today.

They came with clubs and chains.

They came with threats and fearfulness.

They came to take away the goats,

the grain, the metal cooking pots,

the water jars, the tents, the simple tools.

They came with scorn and mockery.

They came to take the dead child from her back

and throw him in a pit of human waste.

Her, they said, they would kill today,

but leave her there to die from all her grief.

FOUR.

Papa Me, who Topside watches all,

sees how my Beloved stirs again.

And rising from her fitful sleep,

each dawn on dawn, has trailed

her hands through riches and

abundant wealth cascading down

from all that Tabernacle of the Earth

    We know as AFRICA.

Whilst we are still a great way off,

we heard them singing their

triumphant songs;

the money changers

and the counting clerks.

Let them rejoice!

Their ledgers cannot save them

from the Reaper yet to come,

whose time cannot be reckoned

by the seasons, but by the One

who drove them from the Temple,

    to where the Angel

    puts the sickle in.

Until the Sanctuary shall echo praise,

there lies another harvest to be won.

Yet, if the gleaners

rise not from the dead:

the hungry and the maimed,

the wretched poor,

the widow grieving

for her murdered child,

whom shall there be to gather up

great riches scattered still upon the

Holy Ground of Africa?

AFRICA -

The Harvest yet to Come.

ASHES.

A fire dies, the embers lose

the red glow of their lives;

a blaze that once threw sparks

into the air, collects them in again

as ash to settle in a place

not of their choosing, until a wind

will further gather them to some

uncertain end, as do my thoughts;

when also crushed to dust,

to ash, to flung on that same air,

we united are become of what remains.

DENIAL.

Slow moving are the Glaciers of Time:

    I did not Sin.

The Cities of the Plain are washed away:

    I did not Sin.

Great Babylon has fallen in decay:

    I did not Sin.

She gathered water from the well:

    I did not Sin

My hands went eagerly about their work:

    I did not Sin.

She has not triumphed over me:

    I did not Sin.

THE GARMENT.

It came to me as my inheritance;

a swaddling cloth once worn

by one who bore it all before

as heaviness, as yoke, as shawl,

as tattered shirt torn from his back;

as one betrayed because of innocence,

as one ignored or mentioned

in reluctant prayer,

as doubted and uncertain Holy One;

but still so generous of hand,

the garment grew

with my impenitence.

...

I was a stranger and you gave me

your addictions, your infidelities,

your wickedness, your lack of faith,

your harsh dismissals and contempts;

with you, amid the downfall

of your temple, I too mourned aloud

and turned away from remedies.

For punishment, God gave to me

a share in this, his sufferings:

these daily lashings on his wounds,

this too, the long chastisement of his love,

and even this, the plague of his forgiveness.

The flood has come and will destroy

in all of us our tricks and vanities.

A great wind roars;

a great wave rises up to crash

upon the shore, changing rock to sand,

and moving it to where the ocean

finds a better usefulness?

No, it is a tide come slowly in,

recedes and then returns;

returns to wash aside each stubborn

doubt and drag all creatures who reside

in troubled pools, towards the undertow

of God`s persistent seas.

THE NINE DAYS OF St. ANTHONY.

Long have I loved thee,

all the desert spaces,

for you have hidden me

from enemies, and in

full view displayed me here

unseen before the all of them.

Enrobe me and enfold me too,

open unto me the door of sanctuary,

as cloud rise over me and summon

me that I may feel the warmness

of your breath upon my wavering,

a draught of love poured out for me.

From whence so many wrathful

furies come to me; this mad,

demented and emaciated breed

of beings dance the saraband

of Sheol`s dismay, enraged against

their banishment and lost tranquillity.

A basket made of rushes is not prayer,

nor is the weaving of a sleeping mat

an act of worship; call all things

by their given name,

and by the honest working of

your hands construct humility.

...

In this desert journey of the night

there are no roads, no finger posts,

skills of the cartographer

are unknown here, and yet we are

not moved about uncaringly

upon a land bereft of travellers.

A prophet, stifled and made dumb

among the last profundity of sand.

   Abba, give me a word,

     lest I too have

   journeyed here in grace

to ponder only on your silence.

Our days are gentle now and

peopled in a land of blessedness;

footfalls pressed into the sand

retain their shape, no wind

disturbs nor wadi alters them;

vipers all are kind and dogs considerate.

It is the nature of expected things

that we have fixed our eyes

upon a door about to open;

no enigmatic wait, no mystery,

a door will swing aside

and our beloved sister sit with us.

...

Abba, does the lion lead the ass

to pasture, do savage beasts

bring water from the well,

in their peace do serpents

share your cave, and ravens

bring you food at eventide?

Let it be so, and may

all mention of the Fall

be heard no more;

the fertile fields of Heaven

are restored on Earth.

THE BIRTH STONE.

And some have said the birth stone

of the world first came to be,

because a huge gigantic bird, which might

have been a Roc or even bigger, retched

and vomited and dropped it from its mouth.

Not knowing what it meant or what to do with it,

men worshipped it, the stone.

Other men, who called themselves the wise,

dressed themselves in robes and garlands rich

in vegetation and thus became a priestly caste,

that they might better mystify the world

with chants and rituals.

...

And some have said the birth stone

of the world first came to be, because

a huge, gigantic fish, which might have been

leviathan or even bigger, retched and vomited

and dropped it on the shore. Not knowing what

it meant or what to do with it, and thinking it to be

a gift of grace, men worshipped it, the stone.

Then other men, who called themselves the wise,

dressed themselves in cast off shells and garlands

made of kelp. They said they had become a

priestly caste, whose chants and rituals would

set aside the need for them to give an explanation.

And some have said the birth stone

of the world first came to be, because

a camel strained it out and dropped it

from between its legs onto the sand.

Caravans had come from minarets and towns,

across great dunes and wadis filling up with

sand for lack of rain, so men might muse

upon what it might mean, the stone.

A priestly caste, who called themselves

the wise, declared that mysteries upon the wild

must stay unknown. The desert all about them

knew its own, they said.

...

Others said, the great bird had returned

to peck the stone so hard it split in two.

Out, as from an egg, had come a golden

disc, divinity in radiance and power.

An edict from the priestly caste decreed

this mystery of light be worshipped and adored.

Who knows, but from its golden blaze what

graces yet might flow on those who will bow down.

On those who worship not, a torment

of aridity and thirst befall them, as of desolation.

Some held, the great bird had returned

to peck the stone so hard, it split in two.

Out of it, as from an egg, had come a

radiance of lesser light. The priestly caste

declared this lesser light must be adored.

From its silver face, great smiles of bounty

yet may fall on those will bow down before

its spells and witchery; a simple lifting up

of hands, a prayer of invocation bring about

an opening of gates, new worlds of rich

enchantment lie awaiting. On those who worship

not this lesser light, will come an opening

to torment, to deceit, to madness never ending.

...

Some held, the great bird had returned

and pecked the stone so hard, it split in two.

Out, as from an egg, had come the countless

fortune telling stars. A priestly caste, who said

they were the wise, declared that here

are stars a man might steer by. From here, they

said, had come the sanctions and commands for all

that men might do or say, or essay to believe.

Each minor pinprick of perfection drawing forth

such edicts and decrees as would direct the deeds

of all who call themselves the chosen of the stone.

Few were those who said that, when

the earth stone had split open like an egg,

on wings of power full formed

had flown a white great horse. Its head was

crowned with laurel leaves, and on its back

a girl who did not smile. Neither did she sing

nor tell her tales. She listened. She motioned

with her hand and bid about her from the air,

soft songs and spoken verse. Ghosts of suitors

came and went as in a doleful dusk.

Few praised her or spoke the well of her. Others

cursed and wished for last release. Some sang

short. Some sang far too long. On all she made

disdain, but back they came and back.

No rebuke of hers could silence one of them.

.

...

Men of priestly caste

who dressed in robes, who walked aloof,

who solemnly processed in varied vegetation,

who called themselves the wise,

found nothing then to sing, or chant,

or bleat into the air such words

not met with scorn and mockery.

END.